SONG OF A LIVING ROOM

AHSAHTA PRESS

The New Series

NUMBER 30

SONG OF A LIVING ROOM

BRIGITTE BYRD

AHSAHTA PRESS

BOISE STATE UNIVERSITY • BOISE • IDAHO • 2009

Ahsahta Press, Boise State University
Boise, Idaho 83725
http://ahsahtapress.boisestate.edu
http://ahsahtapress.boisestate.edu/books/byrd2/byrd2.htm

Copyright © 2009 by Brigitte Byrd
Printed in the United States of America
Cover design by Quemadura
Book design by Janet Holmes
First printing September 2009
ISBN-13: 978-1-934103-08-1

Library of Congress Cataloging-in-Publication Data

Byrd, Brigitte.
Song of a living room / Brigitte Byrd.
p. cm.—(The new series ; no. 30)
ISBN-13: 978-1-934103-08-1 (pbk. : alk. paper)
ISBN-10: 1-934103-08-X (pbk. : alk. paper)
I. Title.

PS3602.Y73S66 2009
811'.54—DC22
                    2009014627

ACKNOWLEDGMENTS

Grateful acknowledgment is made to the editors of the following journals in which some of these poems first appeared, sometimes in earlier versions: *Bitter Oleander:* "(depending on the purpose of a jaded perception)," "(it was not clear as it was)"; *Coconut:* "(conveniently time came for a new rehearsal)," "(the attraction overturned the resemblance)," "(she was often crippled by a drumbeat in the ear)," "(when it came to interpretations)"; *CAB/NET:* "(perhaps there was a beginning to extend)," "(something like *nobody coming* something like *went instead*)," " (how to call forth the empire at the rescue of lyricism)"; *Columbia Poetry Review:* "(perhaps the reason was really that)"; *Fourteen Hills:* "(there was no time to analyze)," "(perhaps it was more fitting than wearing a blue dress)"; *Lilies and Cannonballs Review:* "(how the myth was flattened)," "(when time came to spare his angle in the rain)"; *Mississippi Review—The Prose Poem,* special issue ed. Julia Johnson: "(how to cure the appendix)," "(how to delineate the furtive)"; *Online Writing: The Best of the First Ten Years* ed. Doug Martin and Kim Chinquee: "(the attraction overturned the resemblance)"; *Order and Decorum:* "(a brittle day passed by)"; *Quarter After Eight:* "(how to sink the surface)," "(the way he stumbled on air)"; *Women Studies Quarterly (WSQ)—The Sexual Body,* special issue edited by Kathleen Ossip: "(perhaps there was no concern)"; *The Rose Metal Press Field Guide to Prose Poetry: Contemporary Poets in Discussion and Practice* ed. F. Daniel Rzicznek and Gary McDowell: "(after contemplating wintering in water)," "(how to unravel an obscure bath house)," "(how to sink to the surface)."

CONTENTS

EVERYTHING WAS IN PLACE

TO KEEP THE THEME INSIDE THE STORY

SHE STEPPED OUT BAREFOOT ON PAPER

NOTES 77

TO CARRIE AND RYAN,
AND TO CAMILLE, ALWAYS

Life is not to be conceived on the analogy of a melodrama in which the hero and the heroine go through incredible misfortune for which they are compensated by a happy ending.

—*Bertrand Russell*

Sometimes I realize that if writing isn't all things, all contraries confounded, a quest for vanity and void, it's nothing. That if it is not, each time, all things confounded into me through some inexpressible essence, then writing is nothing but advertisement.

—*Marguerite Duras*

It's just French rock'n' roll
It's just French rock'n' roll

—*Black Box Recorder*

SLIPPING INTO A CELTIC KNOT

Despite his attempt at rewriting the opening scene her Georgian film took a tragic welcome. She had almost reached the vanishing point when he broke. And then there was a tremor in his chest and he pointed at nothing to say there is something broken and she loved him. There. Though thoroughly convincing it was his dramatic dialogue which aroused the commotion in her lyricism. She stumbled on his architectural syntax and held on to her ending. He indulged in peripheral sympathy. His questions made it into the narrative. On the occasion a sensual allure sparked their sexual uproar. There was a furtive glance at his eyes a shifting of hands on her thighs a conceptual prologue to. In other words her show split into a new opening and there was a straightforward wait in the adaptation of their domesticity. *There is of course the bag. . . . There will always be the bag.* After leaving this performance red as his guitar they went on threading through the plot like under-written players.

(PERHAPS THERE WAS NO CONCERN)

That she once witnessed a collection of poets in an eyedrum does not mean her landscape had turned. Their words showed a certain vintage point of view like origami and dexterity. To be perfectly honest his feet were cold and they stopped to eat. This is the way it went. First a glance at the cusp of modernity then a detour by the subset of serenpidity. There was no restraint when natural virtuosity skateboarded on his tongue. There. A postmodern duo with fleeting sadness. She came. With a disruption an opened design an inversion of letters a suicidal punctuation. His was not an architectural quandary. He said *There is latitude in your typeface*. She had caught the bulk of his aesthetics by casting a blue outline on his paragraphs. In theory it was the second day of December. It was just like being undressed. It was just like loving what they were doing with their bodies. It was just like sitting in a car to ride through the sordid. For a moment she had the notion of a poem. He plugged in his guitar and she crossed her legs. What else could they do amidst this stripped hour. His heart was naked and she said *My eye is killing me*. There was nothing to remove from this philosophical evening. The focus had shifted to the smell of coffee and she liked the sound of his voice on her skin.

There was no way out and it was a striking reversal of ideological montage. He said you like knees and she found her hand on his. Like that. Like an authentic vision. Like slipping into a Celtic knot. Like a new perception of space. There was a breath on her skin and time went by. She could not resist the beauty of. This fractured setting confused her when she watched him in high definition drama. *Parfois ta confusion des genres a vraiment quelque chose de barbare.* He stretched his emotional extravagance into a modern scene. The reason was very quiet. She entered her burning with artifice. *There is always the body.* About the scar he said *It's right here* and the story was written on his side like a flower. She watched their slippage like an inward astronomer on the evidence of pain. There was no music. She woke up to feel their fingers locked and there was no arbitrariness in this moment.

Complete with auspicious conversation they performed expansive arm movements to skip the tragic. She said *I'll read you a story*. He said *C'est l'enfer dans ta chambre*. There was meticulous randomness in this nocturnal exchange. They had to confront his lack of balance and the diagonal was inflamed. It was not a matter of manipulation. There was no casualty. She read *Souviens-toi qu'on n'est pas dans un western*. Historically she was correct. Being relocated to a suburb did not change their repartee. She pushed the notion of connection by movement and stepped out. Compared with stringing yearning it was a global emotion. For instance there was a yellow light there was a blue painting there was the Orthodox Church. There. The more he spoke the more she was up for anything. *This uncertainty is taking me over*. The form provided the illusion of plenitude. Was there an open space in this radical choice. She waited for the next image of beauty and his hands acknowledged a discrepancy in time. After he went back for another cigarette she concluded on his sense of logic and drew him back into her.

There was a shift in desire and she sat in bed with the sound of flowers. Was this an exponent of language this dramatization of her heart. He hit her weakness like a keyboard. *Always a skipped note in this cold song.* The level of fascination rose up and the original plot stretched toward a Nomi song. She stood in red ski socks and sparkling silver gloves when there were no more questions about the obviousness of their dreamscape. There. A glorious drunkenness in static tableaux. *No tremor, no perspire: Heaven is here in Minneapolis.* On the other end Henry was still a cat. No reason for suspicion. *It is strange* he said *this melting story.* She said *You have the calm symmetry of an occasional reason below.* He fell on her like a moral emergency and the path turned. Convulsive. Like beauty. Like his voice. There was a retrospective act of manufactured oddity. There was his dream. There was her hand. There.

THERE WAS ABSENCE IN THEIR BALLAD

The following morning she had grown. There was futility in the narrative and her voice broke. It was a challenge. Like the continuity of a fallen history like her eyes locked into his like his body locked into hers like the fear of. *Elle est dehors, la Vie, avec ses balançoires, ses alcools et ses monstres.* It was not a theatrical gesture this leaping out a window it was poetic industrialism it was gauche surrealism it was referential anguish it was just uninspired. She hung over the clashing format of a limb-crushing performance and his early desire clutched to paradoxical pleasures. The question was not her emotional modernity. The question was not the crumbling of the Georgian landscape. He sensed her resistance to shambling close-ups and there was absence in their ballad.

With sparkling melancholy she abandoned the idea of. There was a sense of distraction and he wandered toward the irresistible. *Pas de pensée. Pas de conscience. Pas d'âme.* Trays filled with spontaneous lines like poetic sculptures like romantic landscapes like luminous simplicity. She touched his knee and it was an example of her consistency. In other words it was not a coincidence this attraction to. Ethereal composition original groove anchoring resonance. What were they thinking when they landed in Texas. He said *Souviens-toi qu'on n'est pas dans un western.* Men walked back and forth wearing green beaded necklaces and it was confusing. They were not the same in this catalytic corridor. The writer in her patched this late winter fantasy with a claustrophobic summary. She said *If they let cowboys in they'd lasso us and do you want to miss our flight?* It was a place where meaning was spare and presidential.

(DEPENDING ON THE PURPOSE OF A JADED PERCEPTION)

Organized by silhouettes her undergarments took a blue hue and he followed her European style. There was no safer path. She pulled him through a gap to watch the retrospective of futuristic snapshots and there was no overhead in the room. It was a dark motion toward. *Maintenant jadis est jadis maintenant.* O modern poetry this design belonged to her unyielding gaze. A conceptual set an execution a change of heart. Where were the rodeos of inventive couture in this Southern desolation. Occasionally he expected her to love the sound of mushrooms. He was after all a philosopher. She did not say this was a moment of extreme boredom when she saw his hair black like an emotional challenge. She stood with her back against the wall and his lips against her thigh. There was always a tumultuous context when she came.

To find a corner of splendor was not always a poetic thrust in her severed beginnings. She called upon his flowing mouth and there was always a chance for decay. He saw her as a chest full of classical climaxes and was it not a commodity. Like shipwrecks of obedience like elevators of eloquence like polemics of convenience. She looked for glowing desire and stumbled on didactic illusions. *The earth is very tight today, can it be I have put on flesh?* She shot herself with confusion. There was an edge to her decorated fear. How was he to hug her whirling wants without swaying away from his medicated core. He thought eternal return. He thought mathematical trouble. He thought irrecoverable combination. He chose complacency. She wrote *Did you not hear me screaming for you?* There. No omnivorous communication with the old style. He fed on persistent yellow flowers. She fed on his breath. Until. She crawled over his punctuated past. Until. There was a splintered shadow on her ceiling and she knew. He had turned. She held her bleeding mind like a dream and shouted floral nonsense. Turned. Back to a green wall he missed her wounded lips. *O inessential environment, litter the cathexis of my gyrating interior.* He gave her a recording of his voice and she was too busy to live happily ever after.

Was this a dramatic oscillation when they displayed equally confused romantics at their first spring showcase. When his headlights stole through her blinds she read *Que faire des vieux délires enkystés dans l'âme?* O chromatic room there was a blend of fracture revivals and verbal accidentals in her musical. After she slipped on her red dress to hang in velvet air. After she stitched up wretched balconies into a word map. After she said *All my friends are writers.* After he said *Illusions* and nothing. There was a striking vulnerability in his evaporated collapse. Like a touchstone illuminating her compositional resonances like an anchor reeling her back from choreographed fantasies. There. He opened her onto unbreakable graciousness and she did not have an allergic reaction.

INTO AN IMAGINARY SWING DOOR

After breaking from autobiographical writing the direction pointed to the same passage. There was no moonlit personality no illustrated retrospective no whimsical obsession on this April day. She moved onto a Cubist chapter when he reorganized his landscape with Chinese whispers. She said *There is the trace of a morphing allegory in your birth date*. He said *My notebook does not exude exactitude*. Was this a swarming sequence to. Though a voice signal often leads to dramatization she took a picture of her dog. There was no movie to watch. There was immediacy. There. Like structural pathos like leaking fantasy like narrowing hours in the hollow of his room. A full-scale flying tale made her head spin and he grounded her words in his chest. He said *If you are to paste more images to the story there is always the aquarium*. She thought golden sardine and said *C'est vraiment trop atroce la vie de poisson de banc!* He thought the heart is a lonely hunter and did not say anything. There was nothing on the drafting table when they hung up the phone.

Perhaps they had wondered why there was a nipple on her ceiling after he dropped in like an unsustainable spell. It was another Tuesday night and there was no answer. He said *We sleep in the bed of the inquisition* and it was very small. It was most singularly a joke to locate in this unreliable picture. She said *My fear is only fifteen years old* and they both knew she could not subtract in English. Her eyes swelled when an extraordinary curb sectioned his heart. There was no opera version for this classical tragedy. Next door nothing happened. There was no storm either. She outlined a star and kept its sound under a stone. What else could she do when he wanted a new tattoo. She licked the blood off his ear and it was quiet. O where were her episodic eloquence her artificial imitations her narrative tendencies. He said she was not his mother and she did not want anymore coffee. She said *Is it not yet time for my pain-killer?* There was a need for self-deception in this exchange. He said *I'm your mother* and it was not easy to figure out their parents on that structural night in Georgia.

The colors were set. There was yellow. There was red. There was an oversized heart to drag like a dead limb. In this questionable composition an officer stopped her and she said *All this misery afflicted my driving and I could not pause at the light*. The conflict simmered into a prolific twist. Unlike an abandoned underline. Unlike a smoldering biography. Unlike a two-day engagement lock-in. *On parle toujours de la clef du problème, on ne parle jamais de la serrure*. Hers were high improvisations for a shift in focus. There was blood on his fingers when he said it was not over. With so many catalogues she knew what was forthcoming. She had another shot at lucid aesthetics since she was a productive poet. *A collaborative process often ends in a new proposition*. Their abandon met head-on and no one declined. Clearly the idea of social relevance had not altered his sentences and she permeated the implications. The impulse was to hit her keyboard and never end the narrative.

Everyone knew that in the end their story was nothing like a digital disregard for the present. A change in the concept of essential dialogue required an injection of emotional urgency with a dash of blue and what was heavier than his voice. She said *What was wrong with the other one?* He said *Atlanta*. There was no shift in his composition. Only she was sitting on the countertop. Like that. Like a slice of bread. Like an empty glass of wine. She placed his fingers on her lips and did not eat them. It was not *L'Âge d'or*. He did not kick her dog. He did not say *C'est logique* —*Because I have made my love drunk / with an astringent sadness.* On the other hand the thought of a sequel did not come up and there was a great sense of justice outside the kitchen. Since little was known of the past they moved on to another room.

Back in the kitchen the appearances did not praise her asymmetric perspective on high architectonics when she reached the clouds. There was always industrial farming below. There was always an illusion of abundance. And. There was always faith when detached body parts performed in bright lights under cellophane sheets. *Tous les animaux ne peuvent pas être fous comme le peuvent les hommes*. The question was not whether she could make a perfect flan anymore. Not surprisingly her mind swept across the appliances through past duets into an imaginary swing door until. He wheeled his way to her with yellow flowers tied to a tripod. *I am what I was, / but a man came to me*. The line-up for this precarious installation catapulted her into a poem without a hero and she called him. *How else do you read your heart from a dog-eared corridor?*

The answer was then a sprawling explosion of music since there was nothing like a jump back into the thirties to fill the page with words dancing a continental dance and she did not know the steps. He said *I tried the Sheik of Araby and it was hard.* She said *I remember him and he was not that old.* There was confusion in the translation of their sentences. They found a persuasive moment on the other side of a scream. It was not a world première it was about everything that crossed her mind. Like a romantically inclined headless queen like a lyrical philosopher in a stormy suit like a jealous dog biting into an exuberant ensemble. *The thread of this century is made of wire.* And still. The change of scenery hit her like steady drumming and she could not write anymore.

The poem returned again and again with the same guitar and the same violin. Just how empty was her soundtrack was not a careful description of her artistic aims. There was always an illuminating fusion between the familiar and the dramatic and at this precise moment it was Reinhardt and Grapelli's ultrafox. She did not fear the loquacity of their rhythm. She was removed from the damage of the masculine world. She agreed on the premise of a dream. *One day he was strumming on his guitar, and I started to improvise with him*. From this point he was drawn to continuity in cosmic foreboding. Just as the Southern sun transformed him into magnetic irrationality he saw her as Ganesh and it was difficult to embrace the notion of the first sound when she often looked for the first word. She said *We had enough coffee today* and it was a sign of her wisdom and intellect. As a result she insisted on expounding the classical concept of the means of escape and stepped out.

THE ALTERNATIVE WAS CUTTING THE EDGE

There was no way to escape the suburbanite polyphony of. Her futuristic badinage did not always pick up the point and it was often a time to plummet. Basically there was no time to aspire to urbanism before the fall. His efforts at sculpting her summer with sunflowers gleamed with philological manipulations. There was an echo in the exhibition. She projected her text onto his lips and listened. There was inversion indeed. And a certain rendering of subjectivism. Like the provision on vegetable and it was not very delightful. Like the regrettable sound of green beans. Like the threat of a jubilant carrots chorus. Like a despicable snow peas serenade. Like the deafening brutality of water chestnuts even if they were a blundering transgression. She did not extend the imagery and regained her composition with the logic of a philosopher. He said *C'est bien connu qu'il n'y a qu'une logique: c'est la logique.* She said *What have poets, in any case, to do with sin?* Despite the luminous artifice of the frame he focused on her skin.

It was not a complicated matter. Grapes grew very vulgarly while he drove into a new proposition. At first there was urgency in the vision and he avoided the junk yard. There was already an island in the background to intensify his accidental tremor. On the other hand there was a shock wave in her identification. There was no point in not writing when it had become a silhouette. It was on schedule. It was an indigo knot. It was under her skin. He was indelible and she stepped across the room to. The only sound was a possible fatality. They were all painted the same compromise like wives hanging on like husbands in repair like children taking a chance. Except. She said *Maybe you are wounded* since he came down a Georgian sky. After all she was straight from the keyboard. There was a possible thinness about his conversation but he did not remember. He said *It was a mixture of turbulence and seclusion.* It was just like that.

None of her longings led them to mirrors since she had not named their figures. Was it poetic indulgence when she wrote *He tore the violence of images with a slanted clout* and his partition pointed at the aquatic world. She forgot to fit her mask before diving into the symbolism. There was gasping. There was blindness. There was no mistaking. He went on painting until her vision was offset by a new frame. It was not an aquarium and she noticed his black hair on her red wall. She said *I cannot explain this attraction to a contrast* and then. Little of it made sense until they shut the door. He said *C'est joli ce rouge vif.* It was not a jaded perspective on immediacy. It was an explanation. The result was equally Freudian and Marxist.

(HOW THE MYTH WAS FLATTENED)

What was the point of wearing illustrative garments when the street was stripped below. *Might we not try to be beautiful today?* The answer soared in great circles since it was unnoticeable otherwise. To put it another way there was no side-effect. Eventually her eyes fell on a decapitated hog out of boredom and she turned the brutal page without correspondence. The next image was a winter field and she had to step out to sit in the sun. Both places made her cold like resentment. When she went back in the alternative was cutting the edge. She decided on gardening with the dog and writing with the cats. There was no conundrum about it. It was about surviving a summer afternoon in Georgia alone. Nothing like raising lions for the circus or removing the floor to unwrap the topography.

(POETIC IMMOLATION)

Despite an occasional drive into the city she collected her characters from words spurred on the carpet like blue mussels. There was no sea to cross and it did not involve the stability of her strikes. They often made a long sentence since a neutral number of keys were hit in the process. Still. There was a fickle beat in this otherwise tranquil afternoon. When an eccentric obscurity damaged her performance she had to turn off her head and realign her feet. Facing a computer screen every day had stabilized her spine into a curve. She adopted walking at the end of a leash as a way to get around. It was not easy but it was not a tongue twister. Considering the pressure to write she dressed in purple and penciled her eyelids white. The effect was ceremonial and still.

(AT THE END OF DELUSION THERE WAS STILL NOTHING)

Somewhere between a sentimental festival and a clear path to adversity they were hanging loose. It was a fragrant illumination and staged her past with waves. There was no other way to say *This is where I found the way to*. Suddenly remembering a litany of ambiguities she ended him while the daughter sung *Stadium Arcadium*. There. In the middle of a sparkling sunset. In the middle of a dramatic scenic drive. In the middle of a parched sugar cane field. In the middle of a fractured mindscape. In the middle of. There. Her eyes like his like a hit like a muffled howling like a battered finale. *Accouplées, les choses enfantent l'erreur, l'horreur ou la beauté*. She punctuated the daughter's skin with additional freckles since the translation was uncompromising.

It had been a volatile time but she was not missing any limb. On the contrary she carried wings and heard it was a deformity. Like a nipple on the ceiling like his black hair on a red wall like her feet nailed to the plinth. It was an otherwise modern household with a floor to sweep. There was always a burning to look into and he turned over the unexpected on the way to an untouched upshot. Just like that. With another towel to feed another salad to hug another cat to toss another child to fold. Clearly his perception had already tripped her linguistic modus operandi. These were days of great uncertainty unlike the congruence between Merleau-Ponty and von Wright. She said *I must sit down to play American poet* and she played black swan and it was a song. By then the level of drama had reached down a summer rain to unearth her heart like worms.

Covered with his freckles she broke with the past. It was not an illusion. It was not a step into the unknown. It was not a digression. It was just another key. He kept his eye on her glass and it was painful to stare. There was no other way for her to hold his heart in her hands. He said *This is fucked up* and threw it at her like a pitcher like a player like a philosopher. *And it rained all night.* The most predictable shelter was not usually featuring a hyper beast herding a philosopher and a poet. There were teeth to avoid and they longed for a diversion. After all it was time to let her room erupt with free will. She said *Les sites se laissent aimer sans menacer de mort en retour ceux qui les aiment.* They locked the door and did not look for a comparable replacement.

Even in this motionless loop they were lost. The thrill of a road less map was no longer the ultimate adventure. She followed a ribbon of speech to find him but he had already hacked a path through boxes and boxes of her breath. It was the end of summer and the earth gorged on spells of rain. What she did next was as excessive. She folded her mouth in her pocket and paled under the weight of the attachment. It was clearly a metamorphosing moment and her feet sank into the ground. He deserted the knife on his way to her anchoring and settled for a new guitar. There was no point in removing the sound of his dexterity. Around that time her hair bloomed into fragrant tulips and it was unusual. There was no point either in erasing her potential since it was only an image after all. The notion that they were drawn to each other was evidently not the result of a major malfunction and she felt into her pocket to unfold her mouth. She said *What have you found*. He said *There is no time*.

EVERYTHING WAS IN PLACE

(VARIATION FOR MUSHROOMS AND POMERANIANS)

The effect of his enlightening update on speed was seen in her decorative luminaries and she was not even with the band. She said *I can't take the pressure of a key on my ear.* Although she had already cut through the genre with alarming ferocity this exhausted subject was splendid. He was not very discordant after all and even if the steps were confusing there was always a sentence to stab. Evidently it was not how we got the stars it was another story. There was still a man sleeping too much. There was still hope for the end of gloom. There was still a Georgian sky to puncture. There. Everything was in place. He said *First you finish the dog and then you put on his ribbon* and it was not as staged as the original might suggest.

On the other hand the landscape was unmovable and she drove through an expansion of. It was not disoriented languor. It was not realistic stance. It was not biting clarity. There was only her breath. There. Like a loud repetition. Like a scorching recollection. Like an opaque revival. There. Only an empty seat in her fractured vision. *Maybe I will fold the wind into neat squares.* It was hard to follow another man in another car with another daughter with a leak in her eyes. She waited in vain for an explosion of faith but she had to turn left on Ginger Cake road. *I have at times wished myself something different.* She unlocked the door with a throbbing tooth and the earth had to wait to show her its clandestine cacti. Clearly the sound of bleeding hands was not happy. She wrapped herself into chenille blue to suspend emergency and he knew.

They were influenced by their first intention and the American landscape inspired them mostly at night. Once he tackled her neck after she had searched his eyebrows for clues to overcome the gap in her confusion. Once she found stones in his mouth after he had displayed a romantic show of lyricism. Dating the vestiges of her attraction to an incision was insubstantial since she could not see the scar on his chest from this Georgian point of view. Before she envisioned his virtual space into a futuristic installation the phone rang and she ran out the door to nothing. He said *Can't I call you without anything to say*. She said *Ecrire c'est aussi ne pas parler*. Ultimately their conversation was controlled and elegant and what happened to their bodies was never documented. It was like a weightless spatial outline. It was like a loud artistic engagement. It was like a distant interlocking of limbs. The value of a cerebral approach to the unthinkable did not deflate the cruelty of the overtone. *Are we ready to die with the birds for nothing?* He said *It is time for me to send you a new song*. She said *I am writing again*. There was a new execution and they went on existing.

He heard a beat below the uncertainty of the narrative and his first instinct was to keep her mouth on his skin. She had after all a reputation for leaving her breath on mattresses. Like that. Like a contagious typeface. Like a fleeting moment. Like a relentless partition. *Il y a au fond de la musique une mélopée mortelle*. She caught his musical indulgence in time to edit the pitch of a fragile triangle. She got rid of the rumor in the tempo and struck the centerpiece. Clearly there was an opening at the angle but no one was gunned down. She did not say *Ça fait mal à la tête d'être amoureuse d'une voix*. She just painted his words on her neck with the brush of a blue scarf. She just swallowed his name with a spoonful of orange sleep. She just wrapped his heart in a new sarong. It was an exclusive gesture to prepare for the vacancy of the universe. She said *Your generals have mushrooming visions* and it was the end of a poem.

(HOW TO CONCENTRATE ON A BURNING SET)

That a poem ended was hardly surprising in this flight from a cracked narrative. After all it was not a linear lid atop a promenade through her consciousness. It was not a sacrificed scream amidst lonely pillars of flesh. It was not the close of an age of trivial questions. He focused on her decorative tumult and did not say *In your eyes I can see that you fell in love.* His feet were covered with permanence and the effect was relatively passive. She did not ask *Would you wear my eyes?* She just said something about a muse feeding on luxurious Goulash. There. He wore his ears on the side of his head and it was predictable. She tried to fall asleep in the hollow of his unfolded shirt and she did not fit. She tried to slide off his skin scandal and she got caught on his lips. She tried to chew on his lavender words and she broke up in explosive sentences. Was it really too much this confused slice of extravagance hidden in blue notes. It is true that she opened a door and drove past the exit.

Of course she had already alluded to the certainty of despair and it was a place of split survival. Stringing words together in fits of floating sentences she captured the afternoon hours. There was always a collision of images to flaunt. Like a thousand days of inadequate skies. Like fixed yesterdays dismantled by uneven minutes. Like throbbing granite walls wailing in solitude. And there was always a happy beast frolicking like a butterfly. *Et puis brutalement en anglais, il dit: (do you want a ride?)* and she understood how a chenille dress did not fit the intention. He said *Is this a variation on shark skin suits and blue blood?* She said *Would you cage me under water?* Noting the broken locks on her eyes he motioned sunflowers toward her hands. The rewrite was first shown on a screen while the wind shook the leaves and it was not a movie.

When an unintentional emotion fell on her exported heart like a primal sound he showed up and took over. There was enough time to rearrange her character and shape her into a note on the body of his guitar. He tended to her new outline all evening by rubbing his fingers on her back to erase the gap between his words on her mind and her breath on his neck. A departure from the narrative was seriously compromised after he said *Le soleil s'est noyé dans son sang qui se fige* after it rained all day after she said *But look, I want a revolution* after it was like carving up a reference. After all. There was something to say about that many distractions from such a marginal moment. The most pressing challenge was the crumbling of her resonance. On the other hand there was also a stretch in the plot line and maybe they needed a map after all. Thanks to local volunteers the setting was reassigned to this dazzling land.

They looked for an abandoned garden for a brittle hedge for a liquid road. She fastened feathers to her hair into a fickle headband and stitched his sunflowers onto her dress to extend the theatrical. In this overexposed field of poetry he stood like a weather vane pointing at her artifacts. There was always a conceptual pattern to tear down like a fence above the sea. She said *I will gather stars in a plate to feed your idleness.* Back against the empty sky theirs were the only shadows on the competing earth. Clearly this story was devoid of other characters. For a moment she saw the light reflect on his shark skin suit and thought of the lake and the swan and. He said *The sun shone, having no alternative, on the nothing new* and it was from a book.

TO KEEP THE THEME INSIDE THE STORY

Lips red with hushed rush she sat against a mirror and the leaves had already turned across her empty glass. The phone rang like a cymbal crash against the angle of her gaze. He said *This possibility, being gripped, false belief, blind alley*. She said *Brûlure au coeur, poursuite du vent, ne plus entendre, lumière du livre*. They had never whispered their heart-screams under leafless trees and it was a comforting story line on this murdered afternoon. She met a moment of blossoming silence with the dignity of a wounded bird and flapped her wings against the linoleum to break the monotony. Somewhere there was a window open on stars stringed like amber stones. Under such circumstances he flew in with gusto and turned up his symphony.

(RUNNING AFTER A NEW SETTING)

Considering the urgency of their outline on the floor she added an exotic location to the narrative. There was always Romania when their chests could not contain any more doldrums and it was a heartless word like *romanichels* or *manouches*. What she meant was that there were other words like tziganes or gypsies and they often begged the same acceptance. She said *I will follow you to that distant yellow wall and walk barefoot on silent cobblestones*. The reopening of the book did not change the outcome since there was only a page. Clearly someone had to unhinge her senses. He said *Can you see me when I'm running?* and she focused on his empty chair to believe the occurrence.

(HOW TO CONJURE UP A LARGE BODY OF WATER)

Although she limited her two characters to one of each kind she wrapped them with circular sentences to keep the theme inside the story. Occasionally troubled with moments of superimposed composition she said *Ma signification est hors de moi*. He said *A dead poetry is a poetry afflicted with coherence* and the narrative went on with its normal range of bodily and cerebral. She sat under a yellow light to open a wooden box and found his silver sound clutched around a stone. At this point a dramatic transgression in the plot line did not occur since her hand set the lid back on and her fingers hit the keyboard for new words to appear. She wrote polka-dots papier-mâché watermelon-wasteland miserable-miracle and inside her cinematographic longing a sea flung wide.

(AFTER CONTEMPLATING WINTERING IN WATER)

She sat with the sea on her lap in a cold room and a white nest grew in her hand. The sky was blue as usual since she staged primary pigments as a rule. There was no ant dancing on her arms and she warmed up to her role. She said *Show me your teeth*. He said *Shall I come at the same time?* Depending on the accuracy of the narrative it was possible for their words to have stumbled upon each other. Just like that. Just like another vaporous day in Georgia. Just like a yellow house vanishing under red leaves. Just like a dog leaving bones at her feet. She thought of the sound of rain. She thought of his steps in the garden. She thought of nothing else when he opened his mouth.

(HOW TO UNRAVEL AN OBSCURE WASH HOUSE)

When she saw his lips suspended over the landscape her feet slipped on a pair of Beatle boots. She stepped out and the sky was still up above. She felt nothing for its lasting contour in this endless vertigo. It was not long before trees bent under the pressure of his breath. It was not an image of imminent danger grounded in stormy reality. She stood in the middle of the garden without an umbrella and it was a symbolic stance. She wanted his fleeting words on her skin she wanted to be wrapped in hieroglyphic rain she wanted to swallow the sound of space and glow like an illusion. *O substance* he said *il faut donc toujours en revenir aux ailes de papillons!* and her arms spread into fluttering wings. She danced about his mouth like a blue butterfly. She sat on his lips to taste his words. She said *And now the sun may set.*

The night unwrapped in blue as scheduled and she was cold without his breath on her skin. He pulled a string of words from her mouth to weave a winter dress. There was no time to plant new ideas. He said *letting what is asleep become wakeful*. She did not hear blades of grass crash against her thighs like glowing waves. She did not swim across the howling garden like a running fence. She did not dive to find pebbles at the bottom of his heart. She stood in nakedness. There. A splintered tree. A whispering rock. An alarm call.

SHE STEPPED OUT BAREFOOT ON PAPER

(THE WAY HE STUMBLED ON AIR)

After days of rampaging through dreams she noticed a shift in the narrative. The night was broken. The air was accidental. The earth was immutable. In this version of the story there was an obscene sun and her words caught on fire. She said *What else is it but magic, that chasm / between things and their names* and she pointed to his hands on the outline. He painted sadness on her dress with a weeping stone. There was no color on her tossed glance. There was no one on the road either. They took off their eyes to rinse out ashes of sounds and for a moment the screen was empty. He said *Boredom / like an ill-fitting / speech bubble* and went on to adjust her belt. By that time it was clear that she brooded over their setting.

(HOW TO FIND THINGS THAT DID NOT HAPPEN)

In any case the thrust of trees in the landscape kept her sensible when she pulled up the blinds. The sun did not shine. The wind did not blow. The sky was immovable. She sat in bed with a story to illustrate and it was like pushing words into space with a sore shoulder. There was a curled up sound below butterflies hanging in color. There was a silent dog above ground above blue flowers above her legs above the sheets. There was nothing on the sides. She did not say *mais où sont mes chaussures?* She stepped out barefoot on paper. From this imaginary point of view her feet sunk into wet sand and it was not white while waves panicked around her ankles. She ran against the water edges to know where she was. Back in the room there was no action. The phone did not ring. No one came at the door. The dog was still silent. When he did not say *Perhaps God resembles one of the last etching of Goya* she kept on reading.

That leaves split under her feet threw her off frame each time she ran outside to stare at the air with the dog. It was after all an exuberant winter filled with static metaphors. Clearly there was a coincidence between Goya and her family when she looked for *The Divided Arena* and chanced upon Bordeaux. She said *Shall I hurry the denouement for the sun to reset us?* He said *First, I must travel to a colorless landscape and bring you a new dress.* There was nothing barbaric about his performance when she fractured the narrative. There was a distant day. There was glowing dust. There was a glove compartment. There was a flickering note. *Only those who can truly give themselves a burden are free.* The night fell on her liquid like the sea and nothing left.

(SOMETHING LIKE *nobody coming* SOMETHING LIKE *went instead*)

There was always the same half-sunken existence to stare. There was always the same absence to seal. There was always the same departure to believe. There was always the same question to stifle the same silence to trade the same song to play. Same book to open. Same page to find. Last line to break. *How do you explain that?* A yellow flower left by her door. An icon slipped in her bag. A stone dropped in her pocket. Always a note caught on her glass. Falling in love with a voice. His name painted on her eyelids. There. Her return message—*I explain that, Mr Bones, / terms o' your bafflin odd sobriety.* There was always the end of a poem to execute.

(HOW TO KEEP THE HEAD ALIVE WITH FULL ORCHESTRA)

What happened next was a fictitious finale an exercise in departure a stretch of panic. After all it was time for him to stand by her door in red ski socks. She said *C'est ton tour* and went back to her story. At first glance there was a giant pile of snow outside his window and the absence of a Nomi song in his dreamscape got to her. It was like living in a time capsule and it was getting narrower. He said *I carried sparkling silver gloves in my bag for you and you never asked.* From behind the screen she hit the same keys as in Japanese emergency as in eternal removal as in he had turned. What was it already this leaking fantasy this dramatic sequence this French novel. She did not wear pearls in her ears when she fooled around his melting music. It was something like pasting more images to the story. It was something like hunting a lonely heart. It was something like carrying on Henry's confession.

It was back to skipping the tragic by resting on meticulous randomness and she drew a scar on her chest with his drowning words. Just like that. Like a shudder in the narrative. Like the crumbling of his story. Like the sadness of her wings. It was after all the end of the year and when warmth ran out miserable leaves had been the first casualties. She said *It was just a seasonal development and my emotions got inflamed*. Next the plot thickened and he drove back on a liquid road to the brittle hedge of her abandoned garden. Things had come to a halt when she sat in bed with a faithful beast for days and it was time to wash her hair. He said, *Non, ne te laves pas, j'arrive* and it was a sign of his circumference. Historically he was correct and in this version she did not go anywhere.

In this way she was a woman without her hand on his knee. In this way there was a sheet of steel in her hand. In this way she thought moving sculptures to colonize the exterior. In this way she stayed. There. Time went by like a shiny sound and there was no way out. There was only a new perception of the garden. He did not say anything about her slippage. *Knees in the sand. Face in the sand.* About the scar she said *You can read my story with artifice* and he entered her burning. She tilted her head into an extravagant gesture and her body stretched into a Celtic knot. At this point it became obvious that the ending was a modern composition on dramatic repetitions. In an attempt to produce a circular narrative she wrote the last pages with the first pages and he was not the same.

So that it was impossible not to notice that his landscape had turned she pursued the silence between. To be perfectly honest her heart was in her fingers. She did not write about lush gardens and it was just like being undressed. There was no restraint in their late escape and at the very same moment the thread of the narrative had become clear. There was a leg around his typeface. There was architecture in her paragraphs. There was a vintage jacket to suit the setting. She said *I must end the story in a blue string of coincidence.* When he walked in her room there was confluence in their punctuation. He said *quand on est dans la merde jusqu'au cou, il ne reste plus qu'à chanter* and he plugged in his guitar black. It was indeed the first day of the year and she happily crossed that seven. It was just like returning from exile. It was just like finding his skin under her breath. It was just like drinking coffee in bed as a philosophical stance. *Sound of his voice. By my knee. Stripped hour.*

(HOW TO DEACTIVATE A BRITTLE DAY WITH IMPERMANENCE)

Except for that slipping on a sensual allure their film was made of fragments sorted by a poet. The story was set in a Georgian landscape. The plot was built on peripheral snapshots. The characters were at the center of her tremor. There was indeed dramatic dialogue bouncing between gleaming noises and philosophical uproar and wasn't it always the same fence to adjust. She pointed at the idea of grey sky wrapped around her wrists and his eyes shifted to her bare back in a gesture of compassion. He said *Shall I paint a new flower on your dress?* She admired the brilliance of his red stroke and on the occasion the narrative confirmed his graceful approximation of the scenery. She said *Shall we settle on the threshold of domesticity with a handkerchief sandwich?* It was only then that the question of a different adaptation made it into the performance.

On hanging onto a denouement she said *If there is no end to this story I shall tie another flower to the narrative.*

On ending in general he said *Time is running out if you want to buy a horse and your words have swarmed the streetlight.*

On finally making it to the end she said *Can you see a dog jumping through a hoop of ribbons?*

On sealing the deal on a domestic circus he said *But you can't have a horse in Boston any more than you can go out of your mind.*

On waiting for a new image she said *Les corps sont si proches que la vue en est brouillée.*

On making a stone smother the sound of a star he said *I understand each word but I don't understand them together.*

On borrowing what could not be returned she said *Et l'immensité d'un poème illisible se déploierait dans le ciel.*

On painting a red flower on her dress it was something that did not happen.

NOTES

SLIPPING INTO A CELTIC KNOT

"(A BRITTLE DAY PASSED BY)"

"There is of course the bag. . . . There will always be the bag." From Samuel Beckett's *Happy Days*.

"(AFTER GAZING AT THE RAIN)"

"*Parfois ta confusion des genres est barbare*" ["At times, your confusion between genres is barbaric"]. From Monique Wittig's *Virgile, Non*.

"(LYRIC OCCUPATION)"

"*C'est l'enfer dans ta chambre*" ["It is hell in your bedroom"].

"*Souviens-toi qu'on est pas dans un western*" ["Remember we're not inside a western"]. From Monique Wittig's *Virgile, Non*.

"(GOING AROUND THE COUNTRY WITH FULL ORCHESTRA)"

"No tremor, no perspire: Heaven is here / in Minneapolis." From John Berryman's *Dream Songs* (#19).

THERE WAS ABSENCE IN THIS BALLAD

"(PERHAPS THE REASON WAS REALLY THAT)"

"*Elle est dehors, la Vie, avec ses balançoires, ses alcools et ses monstres*" ["Life is outside, with its swings, its liquors, and its monsters"]. From Raymond Queneau's *Saint Glinglin*.

"(HOW TO CURE THE APPENDIX)"

"*Pas de pensée. Pas de conscience. Pas d'âme*" ["No thought. No conscience. No soul"]. From Pascal Quignard's *Les Paradisiaques*.

"(DEPENDING ON THE PURPOSE OF A JADED PERCEPTION)"

"*Maintenant jadis est jadis maintenant*" ["Now formerly is formerly now"]. Ibid.

"(CONVENIENTLY TIME CAME FOR ANOTHER REHEARSAL)"

"The earth is very tight today, can it be I have put on flesh?" From Samuel Beckett's *Happy Days*.

"(HOW TO DELINEATE THE FURTIVE)"

"*Que faire des vieux délires enkystés dans l'âme?*" ["What to do with long-standing restlessness rooted in the soul?"]. From Pascal Quignard's *Les Paradisiaques*.

INTO AN IMAGINARY SWING DOOR

"(THE ATTRACTION OVERTURNED THE RESEMBLANCE)"

This poem includes references to Bob Kaufman's *Golden Sardine* and Carson McCullers's *The Heart Is a Lonely Hunter*.

"*C'est vraiment trop atroce la vie de poisson de banc!*" ["Living in a school of fish is really too dreadful!"]. From Raymond Queneau's *Les Poissons*.

"(IT WAS NOT CLEAR AS IT WAS)"

"Is it not yet time for my pain killer?" From Samuel Beckett's *Endgame*.

"(SPARKLING TENACITY)"

"*On parle toujours de la clef du problème, on ne parle jamais de la serrure*" ["Everybody talks about the key of the problem. No one talks about the lock"]. From Jean-Luc Godard's film *Notre Musique* (2004).

"(VISITING NAMES)"

Reference to Luis Buñuel's film *L'Âge d'or* (1930).

"—Because I have made my loved one drunk / with astringent sadness" from Anna Akhmatova's poem "I Wrung My Hands."

"(TO EXAMINE THE LAUNCH SET)"

"*Tous les animaux ne peuvent pas être fous comme le peuvent les hommes*" ["All animals cannot be as crazy as men can"]. From Pascal Quignard's *Les Paradisiaques*.

"I am what I was / but a man came to me." From Anna Akhmatova's poem "Guest."

"(SHE WAS OFTEN CRIPPLED BY A DRUMBEAT IN THE AISLE)"

"The thread of this century is made of wire." From Etel Adnan's *In the*

Heart of the Heart of Another Country.

"(WHEN IT CAME TO INTERPRETATIONS)"

"One day he was strumming on his guitar, and I started to improvise with him." From Stéphane Grapelli's reflections on his work with Django Reinhardt.

THE ALTERNATIVE WAS CUTTING THE EDGE

"(IT WAS NOT ENTIRELY CLEAR)"

"C'est bien connu qu'il n'y a qu'une logique : c'est la logique" ["It is well known that there is just one logic: it is logic"].

"What have poets, in any case, to do with sin?" from Anna Akhmatova's poem "Poem without a Hero."

"(IT HAD BEEN A STRANGE DAY)"

"C'est joli ce rouge vif" ["This bright red is appealing"].

"(HOW THE MYTH WAS FLATTENED)"

"Might we not try to be beautiful today?" from Samuel Beckett's *Happy Days.*

"(AT THE END OF DELUSION THERE WAS STILL NOTHING)"

"Accouplées, les choses enfantent l'erreur, l'horreur ou la beauté" ["Coupled, things give birth to error, horror or splendor"]. From Nina Bouraoui's *La Voyeuse Interdite.*

"(AND IT RAINED ALL DAY)"

This poem includes a reference to Thom Yorke's song "Black Swan" from the album *The Eraser.*

"(CARVING UP A REFERENCE)"

"Les sites se laissent aimer sans menacer de mort en retour ceux qui les aiment" ["Settings let themselves be loved without threatening in return to kill those who love them"]. From Pascal Quignard's *Les Paradisiaques.*

EVERYTHING WAS IN PLACE

"(VARIATION FOR MUSHROOM AND POMERANIANS)"

"First you finish the dog and then you put on his ribbon." From Samuel Beckett's *Endgame*.

"(PERHAPS IT WAS MORE FITTING THAN WEARING A BLUE DRESS)"

"Maybe I will fold the wind in neat squares." From Bob Kaufman's poem "Perhaps."

"(HOW SHE FELL IN LOVE WITH A VOICE)"

"*Ecrire c'est aussi ne pas parler*" ["Writing is also not speaking"]. From Marguerite Duras's *Écriture*.

"(THERE WAS NO TIME TO ANALYZE)"

"*Il y a au fond de la musique une mélopée mortelle*" ["At the core of music, there is also a deadly threnody"]. From Pascal Quignard's *Les Paradisiaques*.

"*Ça fait mal à la tête d'être amoureuse d'une voix*" ["It's truly a headache to be in love with a voice"].

"Your generals have mushrooming visions." From Bob Kaufman's poem "Benediction"

"(HOW TO CONCENTRATE ON A BURNING SET)"

"Would you wear my eyes?" From Bob Kaufman's poem by the same title.

"(HOW TO MINGLE IN THE SHADE)"

"*Et puis brutalement en anglais, il dit : do you want a ride?*" ["And then abruptly he said, in English . . . "]. From Monique Wittig's *Virgile, Non*.

"(HOW TO SET A SCENE THROUGH SOUNDS)"

"*Le soleil s'est noyé dans son sang qui se fige*" ["The sun drowned in its setting blood"]. From Charles Baudelaire's poem "*XLVII. Harmonie du soir.*"

"But look, I want a revolution." From Etel Adnan's *In the Heart of the Heart of another Country*.

"(AFTER ENTERING THE PLACE OF ILLUMINATIONS)"

"The sun shone, having no alternative, on the nothing new." From Samuel Beckett's *Murphy*.

TO KEEP THE THEME INSIDE DE STORY

"(SONG OF A LIVING ROOM)"

"Brûlure au cœur, poursuite du vent, ne plus entendre, lumière du livre" ["Blister on the heart, wind chase, no longer hearing, radiance of the book"].

"(HOW TO CONJURE UP A LARGE BODY OF WATER)"

"A dead poetry is a poetry afflicted with coherence." from E. M.Cioran *The Trouble with Being Born.*

"Ma signification est hors de moi" ["My significance is outside my self"]. From Maurice Merleau-Ponty's *Phénoménologie de la Perception.*

"(HOW TO UNRAVEL AN OBSCURE WASH HOUSE)"

"O substance. . . il faut donc toujours en revenir aux ailes de papillons!" ["O matter. . . then we must always revert to butterflies wings!"].

"(HOW TO SINK THE SURFACE)"

"Letting what is asleep become wakeful." From Martin Heidegger's *The Fundamental Concepts of Metaphysics.*

SHE STEPPED OUT BAREFOOT ON PAPER

"(THE WAY HE STUMBLED ON AIR)"

"What else is it but magic, that chasm / between things and their names?" From Durs Grünbein's poem "Variations on No Theme."

"Boredom / like an ill-fitting / speech bubble." From Durs Grünbein's poem "Almost a Song."

"(HOW TO SING THE DISTANCE)"

This poem includes a reference to *Divided Arena*, a painting by Francisco Goya, who lived the last years of his life in voluntary exile in Bordeaux, France.

"Only those who can truly give themselves a burden are free." from Martin Heidegger's *The Fundamental Concepts of Metaphysics.*

"(SOMETHING LIKE *nobody coming* SOMETHING LIKE *went instead*)"

"How do you explain that?" and "I explain that, Mr. Bones / in term o' your bafflin odd sobriety." from John Berryman's *Dream Songs* (# 76).

"(HOW TO KEEP THE HEAD ALIVE WITH FULL ORCHESTRA)"

   "*C'est ton tour*" ["It's your turn"].

"(HOW TO CALL FORTH THE EMPIRE AT THE RESCUE OF LYRICISM)"

   This poem includes a reference to Napoleon's letter to his wife, Impress Joséphine, in which he asked her not to wash until he came back.

   "*Non, ne te laves pas, j'arrive*" ["No, do not wash, I'm coming"].

"(PERHAPS THERE WAS A BEGINNING TO UNDREAM)"

   "*Quand on est dans la merde jusqu'au cou, il ne reste plus qu'à chanter*" ["When buried in shit all the way up to the neck, singing is all that is left"]. From Samuel Beckett.

   "*Les corps sont si proches que la vue en est brouillée*" ["The bodies are so near that the sight is blurred"]. From Pascal Quignard's *Les Paradisiaques*.

   "*Et l'immensité d'un poème illisible se déploierait dans le ciel*" [And the immensity of a blank poem would unfold into the sky"]. From Marguerite Duras's *Écrire*.

A native of France where she was trained as a dancer, Brigitte Byrd is the author of *Fence Above the Sea* (Ahsahta, 2005) and *The Dazzling Land* (Black Zinnias, 2008). She received a Ph.D. in English/Creative Writing from Florida State University in 2003. She currently lives in the southern crescent of Atlanta with her daughter and their ménagerie and teaches Creative Writing at Clayton State University. She is also an editorial reviewer for *Confluence: The Journal of Graduate Liberal Studies* and writes micro-reviews for *Oranges & Sardines*.

Ahsahta Press

SAWTOOTH POETRY PRIZE SERIES

2002: Aaron McCollough, *Welkin* (Brenda Hillman, judge)

2003: Graham Foust, *Leave the Room to Itself* (Joe Wenderoth, judge)

2004: Noah Eli Gordon, *The Area of Sound Called the Subtone* (Claudia Rankine, judge)

2005: Karla Kelsey, *Knowledge, Forms, The Aviary* (Carolyn Forché, judge)

2006: Paige Ackerson-Kiely, *In No One's Land* (D. A. Powell, judge)

2007: Rusty Morrison, *the true keeps calm biding its story* (Peter Gizzi, judge)

2008: Barbara Maloutas, *the whole Marie* (C. D. Wright, judge)

NEW SERIES

1. Lance Phillips, *Corpus Socius*
2. Heather Sellers, *Drinking Girls and Their Dresses*
3. Lisa Fishman, *Dear, Read*
4. Peggy Hamilton, *Forbidden City*
5. Dan Beachy-Quick, *Spell*
6. Liz Waldner, *Saving the Appearances*
7. Charles O. Hartman, *Island*
8. Lance Phillips, *Cur aliquid vidi*
9. Sandra Miller, *oriflamme.*
10. Brigitte Byrd, *Fence Above the Sea*
11. Ethan Paquin, *The Violence*
12. Ed Allen, *67 Mixed Messages*
13. Brian Henry, *Quarantine*
14. Kate Greenstreet, *case sensitive*
15. Aaron McCollough, *Little Ease*
16. Susan Tichy, *Bone Pagoda*
17. Susan Briante, *Pioneers in the Study of Motion*
18. Lisa Fishman, *The Happiness Experiment*
19. Heidi Lynn Staples, *Dog Girl*
20. David Mutschlecner, *Sign*
21. Kristi Maxwell, *Realm Sixty-four*
22. G. E. Patterson, *To and From*
23. Chris Vitiello, *Irresponsibility*
24. Stephanie Strickland, *Zone : Zero*
25. Charles O. Hartman, *New and Selected Poems*
26. Kath Jesme, *The Plum-Stone Game*
27. Ben Doller, *FAQ:*
28. Carrie Olivia Adams, *Intervening Absence*
29. Rachel Loden, *Dick of the Dead*
30. Brigitte Byrd, *Song of a Living Room*
31. Kate Greenstreet, *The Last 4 Things*

Ahsahta Press

MODERN AND CONTEMPORARY
POETRY OF THE AMERICAN WEST

Sandra Alcosser, *A Fish to Feed All Hunger*

David Axelrod, *Jerusalem of Grass*

David Baker, *Laws of the Land*

Dick Barnes, *Few and Far Between*

Conger Beasley, Jr., *Over DeSoto's Bones*

Linda Bierds, *Flights of the Harvest-Mare*

Richard Blessing, *Winter Constellations*

Boyer, Burmaster, and Trusky, eds., *The Ahsahta Anthology*

Peggy Pond Church, *New and Selected Poems*

Katharine Coles, *The One Right Touch*

Wyn Cooper, *The Country of Here Below*

Craig Cotter, *Chopstix Numbers*

Judson Crews, *The Clock of Moss*

H. L. Davis, *Selected Poems*

Susan Strayer Deal, *The Dark is a Door*

Susan Strayer Deal, *No Moving Parts*

Linda Dyer, *Fictional Teeth*

Gretel Ehrlich, *To Touch the Water*

Gary Esarey, *How Crows Talk and Willows Walk*

Julie Fay, *Portraits of Women*

Thomas Hornsby Ferril, *Anvil of Roses*

Thomas Hornsby Ferril, *Westering*

Hildegarde Flanner, *The Hearkening Eye*

Charley John Greasybear, *Songs*

Corrinne Hales, *Underground*

Hazel Hall, *Selected Poems*

Nan Hannon, *Sky River*

Gwendolen Haste, *Selected Poems*

Kevin Hearle, *Each Thing We Know Is Changed Because We Know It And Other Poems*

Sonya Hess, *Kingdom of Lost Waters*

Cynthia Hogue, *The Woman in Red*

Robert Krieger, *Headlands, Rising*

Elio Emiliano Ligi, *Disturbances*

Haniel Long, *My Seasons*

Ken McCullough, *Sycamore•Oriole*

Norman MacLeod, *Selected Poems*

Barbara Meyn, *The Abalone Heart*

David Mutschlecner, *Esse*

Dixie Partridge, *Deer in the Haystacks*

Gerrye Payne, *The Year-God*

George Perreault, *Curved Like an Eye*

Howard W. Robertson, *to the fierce guard in the Assyrian Saloon*

Leo Romero, *Agua Negra*

Leo Romero, *Going Home Away Indian*

Miriam Sagan, *The Widow's Coat*

Philip St. Clair, *At the Tent of Heaven*

Philip St. Clair, *Little-Dog-of-Iron*

Donald Schenker, *Up Here*

Gary Short, *Theory of Twilight*

D. J. Smith, *Prayers for the Dead Ventriloquist*

Richard Speakes, *Hannah's Travel*

Genevieve Taggard, *To the Natural World*

Tom Trusky, ed., *Women Poets of the West*

Marnie Walsh, *A Taste of the Knife*

Bill Witherup, *Men at Work*

Carolyne Wright, *Stealing the Children*

This book is set in Apollo MT type
by Ahsahta Press at Boise State University
and manufactured according to the Green Press Initiative
by Thomson-Shore, Inc.
Cover design by Quemadura.
Book design by Janet Holmes.

AHSAHTA PRESS

2009

JANET HOLMES, DIRECTOR

A. MINETTA GOULD

KATE HOLLAND

BREONNA KRAFFT

MERIN TIGERT

JR WALSH

JAKE LUTZ, INTERN

ERIC MARTINEZ, INTERN

NAOMI TARLE, INTERN